Library of
Davidson College

SHAKESPEARE'S SIGNIFICANCES

BY
EDMUND BLUNDEN

FOLCROFT LIBRARY EDITIONS / 1974

822.33
T4fl

Library of Congress Cataloging in Publication Data

Blunden, Edmund Charles, 1896-
  Shakespeare's significances.

  Reprint of the 1929 ed. published by Oxford
University Press, London, which was issued as
of Shakespeare Association papers.
  1. Shakespeare, William, 1564-1616. King
I. Title. II. Series: Shakespeare Associ[ation],
London. Papers, no. 14.
PR2819.B6 1973   822.3'3   73-9822
ISBN 0-8414-3160-4 (lib. bdg.)

Limited 100 Copies

Manufactured in the United States of America.

Folcroft Library Editions
Box 182
Folcroft, Pa. 19032

74-6094

SHAKESPEARE'S SIGNIFICANCES

BY
EDMUND BLUNDEN

1929

SHAKESPEARE'S SIGNIFICANCES
A PAPER READ BEFORE THE SHAKESPEARE ASSOCIATION, 25th JANUARY, 1929, AT KING'S COLLEGE, LONDON

THE DE LA MORE PRESS LIMITED
2A CORK STREET, BOND STREET, W.1

SHAKESPEARE'S SIGNIFICANCES

SOME years ago, when I was for one voyage officially signed as purser to a ship carrying a quantity of coal-dust to South America, I had the pleasure of long literary conversations with the captain, who was a man of considerable reading. In the natural course we made our way by Conan Doyle and even *The Light of Asia* by Sir Edwin Arnold to the verges of Shakespeare. It happened that the third mate and I were both devoted to certain passages in the great tragedies, and kept up conversations largely in Shakespearean tags, such as 'Help! Help! . . . What kind of help?' But the captain, with his steady movement of mind and body, was not so handy with the apparent implements of Shakespeare's appeal to the gallery. He said: 'I must say I haven't yet made much of Shakespeare. I am waiting. Older captains tell me that you can't read Shakespeare until after you've turned forty.'

That remark has haunted me ever since I left him with his chart and his cigar, and although now, if I were obeying the advice exactly, I should not be qualified to stand here and read my essay at all, yet it is the endeavour to recognize why such men of experience see Shakespeare so that has induced me to make my footnotes to some of the plays. I take it that the character of British sea-captains is essentially a resolution to understand a subject in all its bearings, the fruit of actual education at first hand in the ways of ships, the ways of men, and perhaps it would be safe to add the ways of women. They, more than most men, acquire the sense of the deeps of sea, of heaven, of the human heart; they are accustomed to reading the complex in the simple. A cloud no bigger than a man's hand, a new note in the wind, an allusion over the salt junk—and they are aware of 'a number of things.' That sense of concealed but powerful meanings, in hints which almost pass too rapidly for observation, and which must be won, as Melville says, out of the abysses above and underneath, is the second nature without which my old captain was unwilling to take command of his Shakespeare. He realized well, in his particular universe, the practical meaning, the ideal beauty, the traditional fascination, the intellectual importance, the emotional chances combined in one instant; and felt that in the Shakespearean universe there is a similar accumulation of effects, and words and phrases that operate at similar planes of significance.

Cryptography has long since taken up her abode at a spiritual Stratford or St. Albans, and, though the direction and temper of most of the consequent investigations have been ludicrous, there is a sense in which all critics of Shakespeare must be cryptographers. 'A sort of riddling terms' is found in Sophocles; the short and unadorned dialogue there vibrates with additional tragic purposes; no wonder then if Shakespeare, in a country full of proverb, metaphor, parable and pun, is supremely skilful in conducting his characters to their destiny by means of oracular and laconic utterances. For stage presentation, it is very probable that only the external and immediate references of these needs to be grasped. Upon my submitting some instances of what I take to be the Shakespearean sublimation of the pun, a friend of the highest judgment in poetical mysteries observed: 'Very well; but according to your theory Shakespeare's audiences would have to be all Shakespeares.' Ultimately, it might be so; but for the transitions and logic of the moment, not so. In the cinematograph we have a scarcely surpassable case of sheer surface and rapid narrative supplying all that 'the public wants' on the spur of the moment. But even there, what King Lear calls a 'darker purpose' is the secret of continued liking and demand. It is on this account that Chaplin, the Elizabethan of the films, is the only creator of works that can be seen again and again with pleasure. In story and situation the films with which he has captured the world and held it for ten years are swift enough, various enough to satisfy the least thoughtful. But he never fails to include some deeper theme or characteristic which repays more painful thinking. The fight for the tramp on the highway of human society has sustained his work first and last, and hardly a gesture escapes him without strong emotional reason. Consider, for instance, the ending of his recent play, *The Circus*. The wanderer, who entered a world in which romance and even money came his way, and who has left it again as lonely and possessionless as when he began, sits over the ashes; plays with a relic, with *the* relic of the whole episode; crumples it up and casts it from him, and then walks with his pathetic comic peculiarity out of view. But, as he goes, one swift glance right and left, one lively skipping step, tell us that he is master of himself. It is morning, it is freedom, and in that glance we have the spirit of 'fresh fields and pastures new.' Napoleon, or Charlie?

Of this quality, and of unique degree, are the significant gestures of Shakespeare, and without pretending to offer very much that is not already extant somewhere in the commentators, or perfectly well apprehended by every good reader of Shakespeare, I shall now attempt to produce a series of examples of his myriad-mindedness from a play in which he delineates one of his most perplexing subjects. That play is *King Lear*. I do not know that it can be called a study of insanity. It is rather a revelation of the sanity, or inevitable sequence, underlying and co-ordinating what superficially seems incoherence. And, since the play of character, incident and feeling is subtle, attention must be subtle also, even though the course of our curious considerings may make us run the risk of being styled cryptographers with a difference. I begin by noticing the way in which Shakespeare invites us to watch the similarities in initials of tragedy, or the contrasts in things which have the marks of similarity. We have heard Cordelia reply to her father, 'Nothing, my lord.' It is honesty's voice, and it sounds the call for Lear's disaster. Lear plays on the word. In the end of the scene, he grimly answers Burgundy's proposal to accept Cordelia with a dowry.

> Nothing: I have sworn: I am firm.

Already it is a danger-signal. We come presently to the menace of a secondary tragedy, when Edmund is plotting against Edgar. Again, this word: dishonesty's voice:

> *Glo.* What paper were you reading?
> *Edm.* Nothing, my lord.

And Gloucester, like Lear, plays on the word which sets his misery, if he knew it, in motion.

There is a development of pathos akin to this in the high words between Kent and Lear at the beginning, and their echoes in Gloucester's courtyard. 'See better, Lear,' said Kent at the outset, but the answer is 'Now by Apollo,' and that oath being answered again, Lear finally seals the banishment of Kent with 'By Jupiter.' When under very different conditions Lear finds Kent, disguised, in the stocks, another combat of opinion occurs, and concludes

> *Lear.* By Jupiter, I swear, no.
> *Kent.* By Juno, I swear, ay.

There is a pause here. Will the strong candour of this opposition, even to the shouting back of his oaths, remind Lear of that other occasion, and make him 'see better?'

But Lear's thought has receded to original sources, as he thinks them. It was his way from the beginning. His mind, seizing on a notion, is apt to work on that without a chance of being redirected in time. Cordelia's 'Nothing' is followed by a beautiful and complete declaration, ending with emphasis

> Sure I shall never marry like my sisters
> To love my father *all*.

Lear responds, 'But goes thy heart with *this*?' He has not heard. He means still, with 'nothing.' He himself illustrates this fatal insistency in the figure of the dragon and his prey. It becomes a dominant method in his madness to catch up some idea, whether suggested to his memory by circumstances or to his mind by the conversation he hears, and to retain it and shape other matters to it with a kind of pride. This, of course, is readily seen when 'poor Tom,' himself the centre of a tragic whirlwind, comes before Lear on the heath, and Lear cannot discover any other explanation of this companion of rats and rain other than that he too had 'unkind daughters.' That way the summit of his madness lies, but there are other and less dreadful aspects of his iterating to himself one particular theme.

I may choose one prolonged example of these, which has not, so far as I can find, received close attention. Lear, from the first, is portrayed as being a little inclined to remember his school education. His reply to Cordelia's unhappy 'Nothing' is exactly a thesis of the old natural philosophers: 'An Aliquid producatur ex Nihilo?'

> Nothing will come of nothing.

Soon after, with a reference to 'the barbarous Scythian,' he appears to have Horace in mind. He breaks into Latin—'Hysterica passio'—when describing his physical trouble, a 'fit of the mother'; he compares himself to

Prometheus with a vulture at his heart. And in the third act, he listens to the wild account that poor Tom, with his blanket only to protect him, gives of his tribulations, such as 'riding on a bay trotting-horse over four-inched bridges.' Lear listens to this recital of vivid wretchedness, and his mind fastens on the case of poor Tom. Presently he refers to him as 'this philosopher,' and propounds to him a question, not solely suitable to the war of elements all round, but familiar among the ancient philosophers. 'What is the cause of thunder?' Even in this is involved, not only the academic interest of Lear, his notion of 'poor Tom' and the weather, but some allusion to the clash of hot and cold, of his own ardent love confronted with the marble-hearted ingratitude of his daughters. We proceed. 'Riding over four-inched bridges' and other visions raised by poor Tom's autobiography have stirred Lear's recollection of a famous passage. '*Modo* is he called and Mahu' chances to chime with that. The next title he gives poor Tom is 'learned Theban,' and after a little while that is changed for 'good Athenian.' In short, fascinated by Tom's amazements, Lear is all this time contemplating the position through the first Epistle of the second book of Horace, and particularly through these lines:

> Ille per extentum funem mihi posse videtur
> Ire poëta, meum qui pectus inaniter angit,
> Irritat, mulcet, falsis terroribus implet,
> Ut magus; et modo me Thebis, modo ponit Athenis.

'That is the poet for me, the man who can walk the whole tight-rope of his art, the man who distresses me with imaginings, who angers, comforts, fills with unreal horror like a wizard, who makes me be at Thebes one minute and the next at Athens.' So, there is a unity between the scattered eccentricities of Lear.

When this Horatian byplay is still happening in Lear's mind, Edgar chances to originate another stubborn notion.

Lear. What is your study?
Edg. How to prevent the fiend, and to kill vermin.
Lear. Let me ask you one word in private.

At this point Kent intervenes, but we can guess what the question would have been. How did he kill his daughters? Duly the word 'vermin' works; and in the scene in the farm-house later, when Lear prepares to 'arraign them straight,' he addresses the *idola* of his daughters according to its significance, 'Now, you she-foxes!' Towards the close of that scene, he reverts to his caprice of quoting Horace, and orders poor Tom to find some better 'garments'—he had only a blanket: 'you will say they are Persian attire, but let them be changed.' This witty stroke is fully appreciated if we see that it plays on the last ode of Horace, Book First: 'Persicos odi, puer, apparatus' ('My boy, Persian attire and I don't agree').

With poignant chances of recovery, no sooner discovered than destroyed, Lear passes into deeper insanity; his talk then leaps from one subject to another with wilder haste; and still there is a contexture in it. He has now the additional confusion of the rumoured war with France among his principal motives. And so, when he has made his escape at Dover, and comes with his crown of weeds to the side of Gloucester and Edgar, he begins: 'No, they cannot touch me for coining'; the metaphor echoes, and he changes it into actuality, 'There's your press-money.' He is 'the king himself,' preparing his army for the quarrel with France, inspecting recruits. 'That fellow handles his bow like a crow-keeper.' Again we must see not only the fantasy of Lear, but the bird-boy passing over the farm. 'Look, look! a mouse'; apparently a reminiscence of the classical proverb, certainly a Falstaffian comment on a supposed recruit's usefulness, and clearly a remark brought on by his spying a field-mouse in the corn. 'O! well flown, bird,' by no great extension of this, is his enthusiasm for falconry bursting forth as he sees the hawk drop on that mouse. We have from him a picture both of the country circumstances and his life and times. 'Give the word,' he finishes, like a sentry. 'Sweet marjoram,' says Edgar. It sounds 'aloof from the entire point'; yet Lear says 'Pass.' And with good secret reason. Sweet marjoram was accounted, accounted to Culpeper, a blessed remedy for diseases of the brain. Edgar was clearly a friend. Some other oblique significances in this scene have been well displayed by the eighteenth century commentators. Gloucester, eyeless, is speaking with Lear:

> Dost thou know me?
> *Lear.* I remember thine eyes well enough. Dost thou squiny at me? No, do thy worst, blind Cupid; I'll not love.

The final depths of distress indicated by this disinterested jesting would be enough, but Shakespeare's mark is abundance. We are to feel, even here, that Lear is pondering the grossness of mortality; for 'blind Cupid' was the sign painted over the door of brothels. More bewildering still is the accurate inevitability which brings Lear back from his philosophy to his mad hope, as it is explained by Johnson:

> *Lear.* . . . I will preach to thee: mark.
> [He takes a hat in his hand, and turns it about.]
> When we are born, we cry that we are come
> To this great stage of fools.
> [He pauses, looks at the hat; admires the fashion of it.]
> This' a good block!
> [That is, the mould of a felt hat. It suggests something:]
> It were a delicate stratagem to shoe
> A troop of horse with felt; I'll put it in proof,
> And when I have stolen upon these sons-in-law,
> Then kill. . . .

In this manner every circumstance is made an agent as well as an accompaniment of the chief misery; it is not safe for Lear even to look at a hat or a straw.

The country symbolism of flowers, which at length resulted in those little pretty gift-books of the *Language of Flowers*, was known to Shakespeare, and contributed its colours to the full beauty of his plays. I imagine that wildflowers were not so remote from the Londoner's life in his day that his choosing some of them to suit a particular dramatic moment from more than one point of view would pass without appreciation. It is in *Hamlet* rather than *King Lear* that his garlanding of blooms and messages pleases his creative mind most notably; there we have the rosemary for remembrance, the pansies for thoughts, and the other bitterly sweet flowers; there, too, the 'fantastic garlands' that Ophelia has taken with her to the pool are more than the chance companions of her drowning. They are the omens and the ghosts of it. Yet in *King Lear*, also, we are to use our sense and our tradition, too, when flowers come into the tragedy. I have not at the moment the means to explore fully the association of 'all the idle weeds' that Cordelia names as making up Lear's 'crown'—already we see that they carry a meaning beyond that of mere picturesque detail of madness. They are his crown of thorns. But among them the *nettle* that throngs about graves, the *hemlock* with its fame for poison and narcotic, the sickly and usurping *darnel*, can quickly be perceived as speaking to the imagination of the spectator on the elements of Lear's affliction. The same touch, I believe, occurs in the study of Othello, where he calls Desdemona

> Thou weed
> Who art so lovely fair and smell'st so sweet
> That the sense aches at thee.

These rural instants, in colour lovely and in purpose and

association sinister, may well be illustrated from the most exact botanist among our rural poets, John Clare. In his *Shepherd's Calendar* for the month of May, he runs into a catalogue of the 'idle weeds'—there are Othello's

> Corn-poppies, that in crimson dwell,
> Called 'head-aches' from their sickly smell

and there, red and purple

> fumitory too—a name
> That Superstition holds to fame.

'Rank fumiter' is the first of the items in Lear's mockery crown that Cordelia distinguishes.

It will be forgiven me if I transcribe several more lines from Clare's poem on 'May,' although it is not one of his happiest songs of Flora, with the object of testing Shakespeare's significances in *King Lear*.

> With its eyes of gold
> And scarlet-starry points of flowers,
> Pimpernel, dreading nights and showers,
> Oft called 'the Shepherd's Weather-glass,'
> That sleeps till suns have dried the grass,
> Then wakes, and spreads its creeping bloom
> Till clouds with threatening shadows come—
> Then close it shuts to sleep again:
> Which weeders see, and talk of rain;
> And boys, that mark them shut so soon
> Call 'John that goes to bed at noon.'

Now let me revert to the play, and to the moment when Lear in Gloucester's farmhouse is about to rest and save his mind. The storm seems past. The Fool, shivering in his drenched clothes, waits on his master.

Lear. Make no noise, make no noise; draw the curtains: so, so, so. We'll go to supper i' the morning: so, so, so.
Fool. And I'll go to bed at noon.

I do not wish to rhapsodize over these last seven words, but they impress me with their seven meanings:
1. They are a sort of tired ironical joke on Lear's late hours.
2. They make a playful complaint that the Fool would like a little food before going to bed.
3. There is a pun on the people's name for the scarlet pimpernel. The weak-bodied Fool with his coxcomb looks like that flower.
4. But, if so, he shuts late. Surely there has been storm enough during the night.
5. There will be a worse storm still; and at once.
6. It is the last time that the Fool speaks during the play. He presages his untimely death, with a secondary meaning in the word 'bed' of 'grave.'
7. He takes off his coxcomb for the last time to please his old friends the audience.

It is the chief arcanum of the Fool's difference from others that he should combine and encipher his meanings; he is the inspired child, the comical but uncheatable percipient of the true and the false. 'Not altogether fool' is a reserved way, Kent's way, of describing his telepathy. Duly then we find him crying out his paradoxes and snatches of songs, and, since most of them are to achieve the ordinary reward of clowning, the laugh of the majority, their connection with the matter in chief is not profoundly masked. But, when we come to that part of the play in which the sexual ferocity and treachery of Regan and Goneril are revealed in broad day, we may look back and notice that there was one character who from the beginning knew all about the secret. This was the Fool. I will quote one of his hints on the subject:

Lear. Take heed, sirrah; the whip.
Fool. Truth's a dog must to kennel; he must be whipped out when Lady the brach may stand by the fire and stink.

I had for a long time passed this by, as being merely a figurative contrast between the fate of frankness and flattery, when a friend who knows his dogs as well as Shakespeare knew them chanced to read the passage with me, and informed me that there was a latent and unmistakable allusion in it. The persons under the discussion of the Fool and the King are Regan and Goneril. 'Brache' was a 'mannerly' Elizabethan term for she-hounds, both canine and human.

It is in their prodigious ability with cant terms that the Elizabethan dramatists eclipse all after-comers at the huge game of reporting human nature. It is in working knowledge of those cant terms, which even in their immorality have the genius of a strong and spirited race, and not the second-hand smirking pettiness of more recent impropriety, that the older exponents of Shakespeare, Beaumont and Fletcher, Massinger and the others have the advantage of the moderns. Change of manners prevents us from applying the openness of a Francis Grose to all dark sayings even in *King Lear;* but, if we understand the aims of Shakespeare, we shall see the play better in its lights and shades. 'Anger hath a privilege,' and when the deeps of these oceanic lives are troubled, then there must be a muddy violence on the surface. Thence comes the satire and the imprecation on women from Lear. Thence, too, such a detail as where Kent threatens to pound Oswald into mud, and calls him 'you wagtail.' The term describes the self-confident way of Oswald, yes; but more—the wagtail will be seen at such corners as the outflow of drains; more again—it was a term given to the character of a loose woman; and that finally achieves its full meaning in the play when at last Regan challenges Oswald on his relation with Goneril. 'I, madam!'

The character of Gloucester is built up with many touches which are not all conspicuous, and which have the difficult duty of making his tragedy 'his own fault,' yet none the less pathetic, and always distinctly lower than that of Lear. The jovial coarseness in his introduction of his illegitimate son to Kent appears to indicate the worse side of his earlier life. He is included in Kent's equivocation:

> I have seen better faces in my time
> Than stands on any shoulder that I see
> Before me at this instant.

When he comes over the heath in the storm with his torch, the Fool's exclamation is ominous: 'Now a little fire in a wide field were like an old lecher's heart; a small spark, all the rest on's body cold. Look! here comes a walking fire.' And finally, we have to learn from Edgar that the farmhouse, which seemed so welcome a refuge for Lear, the 'dark tower,' held another secret, and was grimly concerned with the making of the tragedy. The eminence of Gloucester is his conscience. He is almost grateful for his affliction:

> If I could bear it longer, and not fall
> To quarrel with your great opposeless wills,
> My snuff and loathed part of nature should
> Burn itself out.

Of Lear we have many incidental characteristics. As has been shown, he is a curious student, and even at his worst times can approach his torture with the calm of a Harvey: 'Then let them anatomize Regan, see what breeds about her heart. Is there any cause in nature that makes these hard hearts?' He is a lover of the English scene, and even as he points to the map he expresses it

> With shadowy forests and with champains rich'd,
> With plenteous rivers and wide-skirted meads.

He is a reader of the classics, and seems when he mentions 'the mystery of things' to have the title of Lucretius' poem in his system; his 'thunder-bearer' and 'high-judging Jove' are of the old poets. In hunting, hawking, archery, tournament, the art of war, and even football he has acquitted himself well, and through his decline lights up at the thought of them. The magnificence of the English sportsman is presented in most affectionate though smiling fashion when, even at the culmination of his tragedy, as he holds dead Cordelia in his arms, Lear catches at a compliment to his mastery.

> *Lear.* I killed the slave that was a-hanging thee.
> *Officer.* 'Tis true, my lords, he did.
> *Lear.* Did I not, fellow?
> I have seen the day, with my good biting falchion,
> I would have made them skip.

'Every inch a king,' he has fallen short of perfection; but he has never fallen short of the desire for it, and under the punishment of fate and age and the wilderness he continues to 'have one part in his heart' that receives whatever may make his rule more equal, his feelings more imaginatively open to the problems of the unprivileged man. In short, Lear is, without 'daubing it further,' as gifted and as generous a sovereign as ever could have the title of the King of Britain; but we must know so much without any illuminated addresses from Shakespeare.

It may be that a closer acquaintance with Shakespearean criticism would have done what my friend the sea-captain's share of it has failed to do, and kept me from botching in my way the trains of thought already dignified by the scholarship of others. I will, however, run the risk of repeating the known or the obvious, while I touch with pleasure on a facet of this play singularly bright with the originality of Shakespeare, yet composed of gleams and glances finely unstrained. As *King Lear* proceeds, much occurs to lighten the movement of the passions and allure the audience along, yet so, that the ultimate darkness must be deepened. One great instrument of this is the season and scenery. At first, this topic is unimportant;

we are indoors. There have been eclipses in the sun and moon, but those can have a chimerical concern with us. It remains good hunting weather, but the plot turns, and the year turns. When Edgar is driven out, he must

> with presented nakedness outface
> The winds and persecutions of the sky;

Siberian days, with beggars' withered arms among withered trees and shaking 'sheepcotes and mills.' When Lear is driven out, the green before the bloom has yet to come; the hawthorn is merely the effigy of bony nakedness, and rain and hurricane seem to conspire to destroy even the seed of life in the mould. Shelter itself is a war on humanity: 'Fathom and half, fathom and half' shrills poor Tom from his outhouse. But this is Nature's last paroxysm. Afterwards she softens, and speaks

> In better phrase and matter than she did.

The human tempest, wintriness and hunger do not follow her example. They become intenser. Gloucester may be blinded, but he comes to the 'chalky bourn' of Dover through fields of corn and flowers; above him the 'shrill-gorged lark' makes music, and below the lazy sea is murmuring, and the samphire-gatherer and fisherman are out and about. Lear may be demented, but he too moves among the ripening fields, and pulls flowers for his head, once unbonnetted, wherever he likes; his eye meets the mating wren and 'small gilded fly.' In his final love-song or hymn to Cordelia, we feel that the sunshine is playing, and the 'gilded butterflies' are coming even through prison bars.

> As it fell upon a day
> In the merry month of May—

the sun goes out, the butterflies vanish, 'all's cheerless, dark, and deadly.'

In making these notes upon the richness, and intuitive complexity, and choral harmony of Shakespeare's significances, I have limited myself to one play, and of that I have done little more than scratch the surface, with nothing like a plough. I fear, too, that such a style of literal criticism as I have attempted may make me seem guilty of shallow presumptuousness, like the 'critic fly' in Thomson's *Seasons*, who settled on the dome of St. Paul's, and decided that the architecture of St. Paul's was interestingly rough. But the points in *King Lear* which attracted me are not roughnesses, but unions of perfection; the mind of the dramatist is such that wherever we are perplexed we are safe in agreeing with the rustic summing up 'the mystery of things': 'It all be done for a purpose'—several purposes.